# PHUKET A POCKET TRAVEL GUIDE 2023-2024

Your Updated and Comprehensive travel Companion for exploring the top attractions and hidden germs of Phuket

JAMES D. FLICK

# TRAVEL JOURNAL INCLUDED AS BONUS

# CONTENT

 **About Phuket**

 Planning your trip

 getting to phuket

 Must-Visit Attractions

 Entertainment and Nightlife

 practical information

# Phuket map

# INTRODUCTION

In the middle of the Andaman Sea is an island of unmatched appeal and beauty, where clear blue waters caress flawless white sand dunes and deep forests conceal ancient mysteries. Welcome to Phuket, the crown jewel of Thailand's southern coast, where vibrant traditions mingle with modern luxury and undiscovered natural wonders beckon the daring traveler.

The pages of our travel guide expand as 2024 draws near to show an exciting voyage through this tropical paradise. The book "Discovering Paradise: A Phuket Travel Odyssey" is your pass to Phuket, where historic temples tell tales of the past and beach parties dance to the beat of the present. No matter if you're a sun-seeking adventurer, a culture nut, or a foodie, Phuket offers a kaleidoscope of experiences that will make an enduring impression on your soul.

Our remarkable journey to learn the mysteries of this island paradise begins in the following chapters. Take a moment to imagine yourself walking through bustling markets where the aroma of exotic spices mingles with the melody of the screams of nearby vendors. Imagine the thrill of diving into the Andaman Sea's clean waters and coming across colorful coral reefs teeming with marine life.

Imagine yourself ensconced in the tranquility of ancient temples, where the scent of incense permeates the space and history is revealed through worn stone.

However, this book is more than just a list of choices and itineraries. It captures the spirit of Phuket, where life moves more slowly and every sunset transforms the sky into a riot of orange and pink hues that serve as a constant reminder of the magnificence of life. Your experience will be as authentic as it is stunning since you will not only discover the well-known tourist destinations but also the secret gems few locals are aware of.

I'm going to enchant you, dear reader. Allow the Andaman Sea's salty breeze to caress your skin and the locals' welcoming grins to warmly welcome you to their country. Allow the flavors of Thailand to dance on your tongue and the rhythm of its music to direct your steps. Every moment in Phuket is an opportunity to create memories that will last a lifetime, so embrace the excitement of adventure and the tranquility of relaxation.

Join us as we explore the heart of Phuket, where the distinction between dreams and reality is blurred and every day is a brand-new travel chapter. Dear visitor, welcome to "Discovering Paradise: A Phuket Travel Odyssey." Your trip has only just started.

# Chapter one: About Phuket
## Historical Significance

Thousands of years ago, in the first century B.C., Indian colonists founded Phuket Town. The region was known as Jang Si Lang (after known as Junk Ceylon) by the Greek explorer Ptolemy in the third century A.D. Although locals preferred the name Thalang, the name persisted for a while.

**What makes Phuket such a well-liked travel destination today? There are several causes:**

Tin and Rubber

Phuket was one of the most successful tin mining regions in the 15th century. For numerous centuries, the tin industry dominated all others. As a result, there was an inflow of Chinese laborers during the 19th century. Even now, their impact may be evident in the food, architecture, and culture. The rubber trade has subsequently supplanted the tin sector, which is no longer booming.

In the latter decades of the 20th century, international travel started to pick up, and Phuket was one of the early adopters. In 1967, the Sarasin Bridge was built for convenience. As more and more people arrived, hotels and resorts started to spring up, and by the 1970s, backpackers had begun to go to Phuket. Soon after, a contemporary airport opened, and by the 1980s, Phuket was well-known worldwide as a top travel destination.

## Trade

As time passed, a number of external factors shaped Phuket. Arabs, Burmese, Chinese, Malay, and Indian civilizations are just a few of the cultures that have come to view it as a significant commercial hub. This was mostly due to its natural resources and strategic position for trade boats.

In the 16th century, both traders and merchants visited the region in search of tin. After a period of time under the control of a French missionary, the British used Phuket as a base. The Dutch and other ethnic groups thereafter began to swarm to Phuket.

It comes as no surprise that Phuket continues to draw a constant stream of international tourists. Every year, millions of tourists come to the island to take in its natural beauty and rich culture. Additionally, the people are always willing to show everyone hospitality.

## Location and Geography

Phuket is located around 890 kilometers from Bangkok on the Andaman Sea, off the west coast of Southern Thailand. With a total land area of 550 square kilometers, it is the largest island in Thailand. Surrounded by several smaller islands, its total land area is increased by an additional 70 square kilometers. The Chong Pak Phra canal, which separates Phuket from the mainland at its northernmost point, is crossed by a causeway.

Phuket has a lot of hills. There are a few peaks above 500 meters, with Mai Tao Sipsong being the highest at 529 meters. These are frequently covered with luxuriant vegetation. Rice fields, rubber, pineapple, and coconut plantations may be found in the lowlands, along with the island's sole large surviving rainforest area, which is now protected as Khao Phra Thaeo Park.

# Chapter two: Planning your trip

## When to Visit

Phuket is best visited between November and April, when the weather is perfect for water sports like swimming and boating. Monsoon season lasts from May to October, and while lodging costs are significantly reduced during this period, the water quality can be hazardous.

### Best Seasons for Travel
### November-April

In Phuket, the months from November to April are regarded as peak season. Lower 80s are the norm for temperatures, and the waters are calm (particularly when compared to the powerful currents typical during monsoon season). However, peak season also ushers in peak lodging costs.

### Key Events:

- Makha Bucha Day (February or March)
- Thao Thepkasattri-Thao Sri Suntorn Festival (March)
- Phuket Bike Week (April)

### May-October

Phuket experiences monsoon season from May to October, which is marked by drenching rainfall, a raging ocean, and perilous rip currents. For this reason, swimming on the island's west shore is not advised. However, if visitors don't mind a little rain and can avoid swimming on the west coast, the 80s on average daily highs and low lodging costs may make a monsoon season trip agreeable.

**Key Events:**

- Visakha Bucha (May/June)
- Laguna Phuket International Marathon (June)
- Phuket Vegetarian Festival (October)

# Chapter Three: Getting to Phuket
# Flying to Phuket

For travelers coming from a distance, flying to Phuket is unquestionably the most common and practical option. The main entry point to this tropical paradise is Phuket International Airport, which provides a smooth route to the island's delights.

## Phuket International Airport

An active and contemporary airport, Phuket International Airport is situated in the island's north. You'll instantly note the well-designed infrastructure and welcoming environment as you step off your airplane. Travelers may anticipate a variety of services and amenities here, including:

Border crossing and customs: Immigration and customs processes at the airport are normally quick and easy. You'll go through the required immigration inspections before getting your bags, depending on your nationality and visa situation.

Transportation Options: To bring you to your final location on the island, Phuket Airport offers a variety of transportation options. There are plenty of taxis, limos, and automobile rental options. For even more convenience, you may plan private transports or make use of ride-sharing services.

Shopping and Dining: There are several stores inside the airport that provide duty-free items, trinkets, and travel necessities. Before or after your flight, you may enjoy both Thai food from throughout Thailand and other cuisines at one of the many restaurants that cater to different tastes.

Airport lounges: Some airlines provide premium customers or travelers with specific memberships with access to private lounges within the airport. These lounges offer a cozy setting for unwinding, complimentary food and beverages, and Wi-Fi.

Car Rental Services: Many car rental companies have counters within the airport if you intend to explore Phuket alone. If you want to take your time seeing the island's less-visited parts, renting a car might be a great option.

## Routes and Airlines

Thanks to a large variety of airlines and itineraries, Phuket Airport has excellent connections to locations all over the world. You'll have a ton of alternatives, whether you're traveling to Thailand from big cities in Europe, Asian hubs, Australian cities, or Thailand itself. Thai Airways, Emirates, Qatar Airways, and low-cost airlines like AirAsia and Thai

Smile are just a few of the well-known airlines that fly out of Phuket International Airport.

Travelers from all over the world may easily access Phuket because to the large network of airlines and itineraries, regardless of their budget or point of origin.

## Travel by Sea

While flying is the most popular way to get to Phuket, water travel offers a distinctive and attractive alternative. If you're looking for a marine adventure, think about these options:

cruise vessels The port of Phuket is a favorite stop for cruise ships traveling through Southeast Asia. Many cruise companies offer itineraries that include Phuket, enabling guests to spend a day ashore seeing the island's beauty and culture.

Ferries: Ferries offer a beautiful and relaxing means of transportation whether you're traveling from neighboring locations like Krabi, the Phi Phi Islands, or other islands in the Andaman Sea. The surrounding waterways and limestone structures are frequently visible from these treks, providing stunning vistas.

Charters of private yachts: A luxurious choice for people who want for seclusion and solitude is to hire a private boat to Phuket. You may choose your own schedule, discover secluded coves, and take advantage of the comfort of a private crew.

# Travel by Land

Although Phuket is an island, tourists interested in touring adjacent areas on the Thai mainland should consider overland transit choices. Here's how you can incorporate overland travel into your Phuket journey:

Road journeys Traveling by car to Phuket from a city like Bangkok, Krabi, or even the nearby Phang Nga may be a fun experience. You'll get to see the various topographies of Thailand and stop at intriguing locations along the route.

Ferries and Bridges: You must use bridges or ferries to enter the island if you want to go to Phuket by automobile. By way of the Sarasin Bridge, Phuket is connected to the mainland and is reachable by vehicle or bus. Additionally, ships run between the mainland and Phuket, offering a distinctive mode of transportation.

On your route to Phuket, overland travel may offer an interesting new dimension to your trip by letting you explore the local region and take in the people and scenery of southern Thailand.

# Accommodation Options

Phuket offers a wide range of accommodation options to suit various budgets and preferences. Here are some popular choices:

# Top hostels to stays in Phuket

## Lub d Phuket Patong

Lub d Phuket Patong is a vibrant and stylish hostel located in the heart of Patong Beach, Phuket, Thailand. With its modern design, social atmosphere, and convenient location, it offers a fun and affordable stay for budget-conscious travelers.

**Room Features:**

- Comfortable bunk beds with individual reading lights, privacy curtains, and personal lockers.
- Air conditioning and fans in the rooms for a comfortable stay.
- Shared bathrooms with hot showers and complimentary toiletries.
- Power outlets and USB charging ports for each bed.
- In-room safes to store valuables.

**Good to Know:**

- Lub d Phuket Patong offers a social and lively atmosphere, perfect for solo travelers or those looking to meet fellow adventurers.
- The hostel is located in close proximity to Patong Beach, shopping centers, and vibrant nightlife.
- Complimentary breakfast is served daily, offering a selection of light bites and beverages.
- The hostel organizes social events and activities, providing opportunities for guests to connect and explore together.
- The friendly staff are available to provide recommendations on local attractions, dining options, and nightlife.

## The Luna Hostel

The Luna Hostel is a cozy and welcoming accommodation located in a vibrant neighborhood of Phuket, Thailand. With its friendly atmosphere, comfortable facilities, and convenient location, it offers a budget-friendly stay for travelers seeking a relaxed and social experience.

## Room Features:

- Comfortable bunk beds with individual reading lights and personal lockers for each guest.
- Air conditioning or fans in the rooms for a comfortable stay.

- Shared bathrooms with hot showers and complimentary toiletries.
- Power outlets and USB charging ports near each bed.
- Bed linens and towels provided for guests.

**Good to Know:**

- The Luna Hostel offers a relaxed and friendly environment, perfect for solo travelers or those looking to meet fellow adventurers.
- The hostel is located in a lively neighborhood, close to local attractions, markets, and dining options.
- Communal areas provide opportunities for guests to connect, share stories, and make new friends.
- The hostel staff are knowledgeable about the local area and can offer recommendations on nearby activities and sights.
- Basic amenities and facilities are provided to ensure a comfortable and convenient stay.

## BearPacker Patong Hostel

BearPacker Patong Hostel is a vibrant and affordable hostel located in the lively Patong Beach area of Phuket, Thailand. With its welcoming atmosphere, comfortable accommodations, and convenient location, it offers budget-conscious travelers a delightful and social experience.

## Room Features:

- Comfortable bunk beds with individual reading lights, privacy curtains, and personal lockers.
- Air conditioning or fans in the rooms for a comfortable stay.
- Shared bathrooms with hot showers and complimentary toiletries.
- Power outlets and USB charging ports near each bed.
- Bed linens and towels provided for guests.

## Good to Know:

- BearPacker Patong Hostel offers a friendly and sociable environment, ideal for solo travelers or those looking to meet fellow adventurers.
- The hostel is located in the vibrant Patong Beach area, close to the beach, nightlife, and local attractions.
- Communal areas provide opportunities for guests to connect, share stories, and make new friends.

- The hostel staff are knowledgeable about the local area and can offer recommendations on nearby activities and sights.
- Basic amenities and facilities are provided to ensure a comfortable and convenient stay.

# TOP HOTELS IN PHUKET

### The Beachfront Hotel Phuket

The Beachfront Hotel Phuket is a stunning accommodation nestled in the heart of Warsaw, offering guests a unique and luxurious beachfront experience. With its prime location and exquisite amenities, it promises an unforgettable stay for both leisure and business travelers.

### Room Features:

- Luxurious and well-appointed rooms with modern decor and soothing color schemes.
- Private balconies or terraces offering panoramic views of the beach or city skyline.
- Comfortable mattresses with high-quality linen for a good night's sleep.
- Air conditioning and soundproofing for a peaceful and comfortable stay.

- Entertainment options include flat-screen TVs with cable.Mini-bar, coffee/tea making facilities, and in-room dining options for added convenience.
- En-suite bathrooms with rainfall showers, complimentary toiletries, and plush bathrobes.
- Work desk and seating area for business travelers or those needing a dedicated workspace.

## Good to Know:

- The Beachfront Hotel Phuket offers a complimentary shuttle service to and from the airport for guests' convenience.
- A range of water sports activities, such as snorkeling and kayaking, can be arranged at the hotel's beachfront.
- The hotel's concierge can assist with arranging city tours, restaurant reservations, and ticket bookings for local attractions.
- The hotel is located near popular shopping and dining destinations, allowing guests to explore the vibrant neighborhood easily.
- Complimentary breakfast is served daily, offering a variety of options to suit different dietary preferences.

## Hotel Clover Patong Phuket

Hotel Clover Patong Phuket is a charming and contemporary hotel located in the heart of Patong Beach, Phuket. With its stylish design, comfortable accommodations, and convenient location, it offers a delightful stay for travelers seeking both relaxation and excitement.

### Room Features:

- Well-appointed and stylishly designed rooms with modern furnishings.
- Comfortable beds with quality bedding for a restful sleep.
- own patios or balconies with views of the neighborhood.
- Air conditioning and soundproofing for a peaceful and comfortable stay.
- Flat-screen TVs with cable channels for entertainment.
- Mini-bar, coffee/tea making facilities, and in-room dining options for added convenience.
- En-suite bathrooms with rainfall showers, complimentary toiletries, and hairdryers.

- Work desk and seating area in select rooms for business travelers or those needing a dedicated workspace.

## Good to Know:

- The hotel is conveniently located within walking distance of Patong Beach, shopping centers, and vibrant nightlife.
- The hotel offers tour desk services to assist guests in arranging excursions, island tours, and activities.
- Complimentary breakfast is served daily, offering a variety of options to start the day.
- The hotel provides 24-hour security to ensure the safety and comfort of guests.
- The friendly and attentive staff are available to assist guests with any needs or recommendations.

## Chanalai Flora Resort, Kata Beach, Phuket

Chanalai Flora Resort is a tropical haven located in the beautiful Kata Beach area of Phuket, Thailand. With its serene ambiance, lush surroundings, and proximity to the beach, it offers a perfect retreat for those seeking relaxation and tranquility.

## Room Features:

- Well-appointed and comfortable rooms with modern amenities and a tropical touch.
- Balcony or terrace in select rooms, offering views of the resort's gardens or pool area.
- Air conditioning and ceiling fans for a pleasant and cool environment.
- Flat-screen TVs with cable channels for entertainment.
- Mini-bar, coffee/tea making facilities, and in-room dining options for added convenience.
- En-suite bathrooms with showers, complimentary toiletries, and hairdryers.
- Work desk and seating area in select rooms for business travelers or those needing a dedicated workspace.

## Good to Know:

- The resort is located a short walk away from the beautiful Kata Beach, known for its clear waters and stunning sunsets.
- Guests can enjoy nearby water sports activities, such as snorkeling, diving, and surfing.
- The resort offers a tour desk to assist guests in arranging excursions, island tours, and activities.

- Complimentary breakfast is served daily, offering a variety of options to start the day.
- The resort provides 24-hour security to ensure the safety and comfort of guests.
- The friendly and attentive staff are available to assist guests with any needs or recommendations.

# Top homestays in Phuket

## Phuket Gay Homestay - Neramit Hill

Phuket Gay Homestay - Neramit Hill is a welcoming and inclusive accommodation option situated in Phuket, Thailand. Designed specifically for LGBTQ+ travelers, it offers a safe and comfortable environment where guests can feel at home and connect with like-minded individuals.

**Room Features:**

- Comfortable and well-maintained rooms with a welcoming atmosphere.
- Choice of private or shared bathrooms, depending on room type.
- Air conditioning or fans in the rooms for a comfortable stay.
- Bed linens provided for guests.

**Good to Know:**

- Phuket Gay Homestay - Neramit Hill offers a safe and inclusive environment, catering specifically to LGBTQ+ travelers.
- The homestay is situated in a peaceful location, providing a respite from the bustling city while still being accessible to nearby attractions.
- Communal areas provide opportunities for guests to connect, share experiences, and create lasting friendships.
- The homestay staff are LGBTQ+ friendly and can provide recommendations on local LGBTQ+ hotspots, events, and attractions.
- Basic amenities and facilities are provided to ensure a comfortable and enjoyable stay.

## Thai Siam Residence

Thai Siam Residence is a charming and tranquil accommodation nestled in the heart of Phuket, Thailand. With its authentic Thai architecture, warm hospitality, and peaceful surroundings, it offers a serene and comfortable stay for travelers seeking a traditional Thai experience.

**Room Features:**

- Thoughtfully designed and spacious rooms with traditional Thai decor and furnishings.

- Private balconies or terraces offering views of the surrounding gardens or pool area.
- Air conditioning for a comfortable stay in the tropical climate.
- entertainment options include flat-screen TVs with cable..
- Mini-bar, coffee/tea making facilities, and in-room dining options for added convenience.
- En-suite bathrooms with showers, complimentary toiletries, and hairdryers.

## Good to Know:

- Thai Siam Residence provides an authentic Thai experience with its traditional architecture and warm hospitality.
- The residence is located in a peaceful area, allowing guests to relax and rejuvenate.
- The on-site restaurant offers a delightful selection of Thai and international dishes to tantalize the taste buds.
- The friendly staff are knowledgeable about the local area and can provide recommendations on nearby attractions and activities.
- Basic amenities and facilities are provided to ensure a comfortable and convenient stay.

# Ice Kamala Beach Hotel

Ice Kamala Beach Hotel is a contemporary and stylish hotel situated in Kamala Beach, Phuket. With its sleek design, modern amenities, and prime beachfront location, it offers a luxurious and unforgettable experience for guests seeking a beach getaway.

**Room Features:**

- Stylishly designed rooms with contemporary furnishings and a soothing color palette.
- Private balconies offering views of the beach or surrounding area.
- Comfortable beds with premium bedding for a restful sleep.
- Air conditioning and soundproofing for a peaceful and comfortable stay.
- entertainment options include flat-screen TVs with cable.
- Mini-bar, coffee/tea making facilities, and in-room dining options for added convenience.
- En-suite bathrooms with showers, complimentary toiletries, and hairdryers.
- Work desk and seating area for business travelers or those needing a dedicated workspace.

## Good to Know:

- Ice Kamala Beach Hotel boasts a prime beachfront location, allowing guests to enjoy the beauty of Kamala Beach.
- The rooftop pool offers a relaxing spot to unwind and soak up the stunning views.
- The hotel's restaurant serves delectable dishes, providing a delightful culinary experience.
- The attentive staff are available to provide recommendations on nearby attractions, dining options, and activities.
- Basic amenities and facilities are provided to ensure a comfortable and convenient stay.

# Chapter four: Must-Visit Attractions
## Phuket Beaches

### Patong Beach

The three-kilometer stretch of golden sand next to Patong is one of Phuket's most popular beaches. There are several boat captains, parasail and jet ski operators, beach merchants, and masseuses who approach tourists who are unwinding on the sand.

Patong Beach is separated from the main road by a shoreline lined with coconut, palm, and tropical almond trees. Beach massage parlors are surrounded by vendors offering food and beverages in this slightly cooler location. Additionally, there are beachside eateries and pubs that serve both Thai and foreign cuisine, especially in the centre of the beach and close to Bangla Road.

A tiny sand creek tucked away in the northern part of Patong Beach offers very shallow, clear water during the height of the season. A river's mouth lies in the southern portion, where numerous fishing boats moor. The promontory that divides Patong from Karon is ringed by a number of coves and beaches, as well as a small fishing community.

Between November and April, when the water is very calm and flat, is the ideal time to explore Patong Beach in Phuket. The beach is subjected to strong surges and huge waves from May to October. On certain days, you can swim, but when the red caution flags are out on the beach, you must strictly abide by them.

## Karon Beach

One of Phuket's longest beaches, Karon Beach is 5 km long and features beautiful, white sand with views of the Andaman Sea. Go to the northern end of the beach, which is normally unpopulated, if you want the beach to yourself. Even while it is more crowded at Kata on the southern end, it is still easy to find a peaceful space for oneself.

The peak season (November to April), when there are the fewest waves, produces waters that are stunningly clean. However, during the southwest monsoon season (May to

October), Karon Beach is subject to hazardous surges and riptides. Despite the fact that there are lifeguards on duty, it is best to observe cautionary signs and exercise utmost caution. By saving wounded turtles and caring for their eggs in a secure setting, the organization's Sea Turtle Conversation Project hopes to increase the population.

## Beach Kata

Due to its mix of beauty, amenities, and activities, Kata Beach, a 1.5-km stretch of golden sand, is one of Phuket's busiest beaches. Each day, hundreds of people come to enjoy the sun and go swimming. This beach is lovely in many ways and is frequently busy but never crowded.

The warm sea is frequently pancake-flat, transparent, and turquoise in color from November to April, when the north-east monsoon season occurs. Although swimming conditions during the south-west monsoon season (May to October) might be tougher, this is the time of year when surfers swarm to enjoy the waves. You shouldn't enter the sea on days with red warning flags because of hazardous rip tides and surges, but on these days, you probably wouldn't want to go to the beach.

The King's Cup Regatta in December, one of Asia's top sailing competitions, draws stunning vessels from all over the world when the waters become calm in the late part of the year.

## Kamala Beach

Kamala Beach: Located on Phuket's west coast, Kamala Beach is a calm and family-friendly beach. In comparison to the busier beaches on the island, it has a more relaxed and calm vibe. Kamala Beach has a lengthy stretch of golden sand and crystal-clear blue waters, making it excellent for swimming and sunbathing. The  beach is bordered by lush green hills, which makes for a beautiful backdrop. Kamala Beach is popular with families looking for a more laidback beach experience. Visitors can eat delicious seafood, Thai cuisine, and buy for local handicrafts at a variety of seaside restaurants, cafes, and shops. Kamala Beach is a lovely destination that mixes natural beauty with a tranquil atmosphere.

## Surin Beach

Surin Beach is an upmarket and attractive beach on Phuket's west coast. It is well-known for its gorgeous blue waters and pure white sands, making it a favorite among beachgoers. Surin Beach provides a more exclusive and luxury experience, with upscale resorts, beach clubs, and restaurants  dotting the shoreline. The beach is popular among sunbathers and swimmers, and its calm waves make it ideal for water activities such as snorkeling and stand-up paddleboarding. Surin Beach has a tranquil and elegant atmosphere that draws both local and foreign guests who appreciate its beauty and luxury offers.

## Nai Harn Beach

Nai Harn Beach: Nai Harn Beach is a beautiful and gorgeous beach on Phuket's southern edge. It is widely recognized as one of the island's most stunning beaches. Nai Harn Beach has crystal-clear waters, fluffy white sand, and a beautiful green hill backdrop. The beach has a serene and unspoiled ambiance, making it popular among  nature enthusiasts and those looking for peace and quiet. The tranquil waters at Nai Harn Beach are ideal for swimming and snorkeling, while the adjacent park area offers hiking and exploring options. Nai Harn Beach is a hidden treasure that offers natural beauty and serenity.

## Freedom Beach

Freedom Beach: Freedom Beach is a hidden gem on Phuket's southwest coast. It can only be reached by boat or a steep climbing track, adding to its exclusivity and attractiveness. The area around Freedom Beach is noted for its pure beauty, with blue waters, smooth white sand, and lush flora. The beach offers a private and  tranquil setting away from the crowds and noise of more popular beaches. Guests can swim, sunbathe, and snorkel in the calm, lovely oceans. Freedom Beach has no beachfront amenities or services, so you must bring your own supplies for a day vacation. The beach's pristine beauty and calm environment make it popular with nature lovers and those looking for a more secluded beach experience.

## Mai Khao Beach

Mai Khao Beach: Mai Khao Beach is Phuket's longest beach, running 11 kilometers along the island's northwest coast. It is a less developed beach recognized for its natural beauty and quiet. The Sirinat National Park includes Mai Khao Beach, assuring its preservation and protection. With soft sands and clean waves, the beach provides a tranquil  and peaceful environment. It's a great place for long hikes, sunbathing, and relaxing in nature's peace. Mai Khao Beach is also well-known as a sea turtle nesting place, and tourists may have the opportunity to see these amazing creatures during nesting seasons. The region around the beach is still underdeveloped, with only a few motels and food options. For those looking for a pure and untouched beach experience away from the masses, Mai Khao Beach is an excellent choice.

# Cultural and Historical Sites

## Wat Chalong

In Phuket's Chalong Bay, there is a historical monument and Buddhist temple called Wat Chalong. While Europeans are on vacation, the natives have come to worship practically every day for generations. Despite going by Wat Chalong more often than Wat Chaitararam, this temple's actual name. On Chao Fa West Road, in

Tambol Chalong's northern section, is where you'll find the temple.

Many claim that multiple miracles frequently occur in the temple. Additionally, it is renowned for playing a crucial and conciliatory role in the conflict between Chinese secret organizations (Angyee) in 1876.

### Highlights of Wat Chalong in Phuket

One of Wat Chalong's most significant Buddhist sculptures is Poh Than Jao Wat. Two sculptures of an elderly man named Ta Khee-lek may be seen in the western ancient hall of the temple. He was a well-known local who, with the help of the Poh Than Jao Wat statue, had won several lotteries. Another notable statue in this hall is that of Nonsi.

A statue of Luang Poh Cham coated in gold is on exhibit in one of Wat Chalong's rooms. It also has sculptures of the former abbots of the temple, Luang Poh Chuang and Luang Poh Gleum.

It is said that a fragment of Lord Buddha's bone may be found in the large pagoda that dominates Wat Chalong. Take your time studying the pagoda's beautiful wall murals, which include several figures and the life tale of Buddha.

The Luang Poh Cham exposition hall is air-conditioned. Along with historic Thai furniture and Benjarong china, it showcases lifelike wax replicas of Luang Poh Cham, Luang Poh Chuang, Luang Poh Gleum, and Luang Pu Thuad.

**Things to note when visiting Wat Chalong in Phuket**

- When visiting Wat Chalong, it is recommended to observe and adopt the residents' behavior as temples are considered holy spaces for the community. It is strictly forbidden for devotees to stand above or place themselves higher than any Buddha pictures.

- Even though Phuket may become rather warm at times, it is improper to dress provocatively within a house of worship. If you intend to attend a temple in Thailand, make sure your shoulders, chest, belly, and legs are covered.
- When entering any of the structures, particularly the chedi and preaching hall, take off your shoes. It's better to avoid wearing your most costly shoes as well, in case someone else unintentionally takes them.

## Phuket Old Town

Phuket Town, which was founded on wealth generated by the island's tin industry, is a historically significant area. The town has assimilated numerous characteristics from the various civilizations that have resided there throughout the years. Grandiose Sino-colonial palaces, Buddhist and Taoist temples, opulent and exquisitely kept store buildings, small cafés, little printing businesses, and art galleries can all be found along its winding alleyways.

Being the center of local activity, Phuket Town is most likely the greatest location on the island to experience "real Thailand." Visit early in the morning or after the day has lost its sweltering heat as it is small enough to explore on foot. There are enough eateries and local markets to keep you stocked with delectable regional cuisine and beverages all day long.

## Big Buddha

The base of Phuket's Big Buddha (Phra Puttamingmongkol Akenakkiri) is around 25 meters wide. Beautiful Burmese white jade marble covers the reinforced concrete body's full surface area. The statue is positioned in the bhumisparsha mudra position (sitting with the right hand over the right knee, extending toward the ground with the palm  facing inward) on one of the island's biggest hills.

From the Phuket Big Buddha, one can see Chalong and the eastern part of the island in a very desirable manner. It's so large that you can see it from much of Phuket's southern region.Learn more.

# Natural Wonders

## Phi Phi Islands

Nothing short of a tropical paradise can be spoken about the Phi Phi Islands, a captivating island located in the Andaman Sea. These islands, which are located between

the well-known tourist attractions of Phuket and Krabi, have won praise from all over the world for their spectacular beauty and tranquil atmosphere.

### The Experience in Phi Phi

A trip to the Phi Phi Islands is like entering into a picture-perfect landscape with turquoise seas, verdant vegetation, and towering limestone cliffs. This archipelago, which consists of six major islands—Phi Phi Don and Phi Phi Leh being the most well-known—has something to offer for everyone.

### Phi Phi Leh: Nature's Masterpiece

A hidden treasure within the archipelago, Phi Phi Leh is an uninhabited island that gained notoriety as the setting for the film "The Beach." Its waters, which are immaculate and crystal transparent, make it a sanctuary for lovers of snorkeling and scuba diving. The underwater scenery in this area is a kaleidoscope of colorful coral reefs and a variety of marine life, providing divers with incredible underwater experiences.

## Phi Phi Don: The Vibrant Hub

The largest and only populated island, Phi Phi Don, is a hive of activity. It's the ideal getaway from the hustle and bustle of city life because there are no highways and a pleasant village vibe there. The lively nightlife of the island, as well as the local markets, mouthwatering Thai food, and the warm friendliness of the residents, are all available to visitors.

## Similan Islands

One of the most well-known island groupings in the Andaman Sea is the Similan Islands, which is partly due to the wonders that lie under the surrounding crystal-clear seas. They are located 84 kilometers northwest of Phuket. This little archipelago is a highly-liked vacation spot for yachties and boat excursions as well as one of the world's most fascinating diving locales.

## Visitor attractions on the Similan Islands

The Similans don't have the same striking natural beauty as Krabi's limestone islands or Phang Nga Bay, which are what most people think of when they think of the Andaman Sea. Instead, you come across low-lying structures that are heavily forested.

Among the bigger trees are ironwood and gum, and the undergrowth is more thick and made up of jackfruit, rattan, and bamboo. Crab-eating monkeys, dusky langurs, squirrels, bats, lizards, and a wide variety of birds may all be found on the islands, however the monkeys are timid and hard for the average person to view.

At first appearance, the biggest draw to these islands are the enormous rocks that line the western and southern coastlines of numerous of them. The white coral-sand beaches, which are incredibly lovely and sometimes uninhabited, are another highlight.

However, the most fascinating vistas may be discovered underwater. The same stones that dot the shoreline are also responsible for transforming the seas surrounding the Similans into one of the most breathtaking coral growths in the world.

## Getting to the Similan Islands

For visitors to the island, there is no consistent boat service. Due to unfavorable weather, boats may completely stop operating during the low season (May to October). The shortest boat ride to the Similans departs at Thap Lamu Pier in the Thai Muang district of Phang Nga province, and takes around three hours.

More daring travelers could try to get a ride on one of the local boats going there, but be careful to leave yourself plenty of time because you never know when a trip back will be available. Note that international tourists must pay an additional 500 baht to enter the park.

Day tours are also an option from Phuket and Khao Lak, with journey times ranging from 45 minutes to three hours, depending on the boat hired. Joining a liveaboard boat cruise out of Phuket is a well-liked option, especially for divers and game fisherman. These trips often last four days. Numerous liveaboard companies in Phuket provide varied degrees of luxury and amenities.

# Adventure and Exploration

## Phang Nga Bay

Phang Nga Bay, located northeast of Phuket, is a spectacular natural marvel that captivates visitors with its limestone karsts, emerald-green waves, and attractive surroundings. Phang Nga Bay is a must-see place for the following reasons:

Phang Nga Bay is famous for its unusual limestone karsts that protrude out of the ocean, providing a magnificent and bizarre background. Explore the bay's many islands, such as James Bond Island (made famous in the film "The Man with the Golden Gun"), Koh Panyee, and Koh Hong.

• Sea Cave Exploration: Take a journey into the bay's unique network of sea tunnels and secret lagoons. Explore the stunning rock formations and vibrant marine habitats of sites like Bat Cave and Diamond Cave by sea kayak or guided tour.

• Panoramic Views: As you cruise around Phang Nga Bay, you will be captivated by the panoramic views that unfold in front of you. The mix of towering limestone cliffs, crystal-clear seas, and lush mangrove forests provides a really unique visual spectacle.

• Island Hopping and Beaches: Phang Nga Bay provides island hopping chances, allowing you to find hidden beaches and snorkel in clear seas. Relax on the gentle sands of Naka Island, Lawa Island, or the calmer portions of James Bond Island and take in the natural splendor.

Visit Koh Panyee, a one-of-a-kind town perched on stilts above the lake. Discover the local way of life, visit the floating market, try delicious seafood meals, and mingle with the kind folks that call this area home.

# Adventure Activities

## Snorkeling and Scuba Diving

Scuba diving in Phuket is well known across the globe and features a variety of dive sites, including vast fringing reefs, stunning drop-offs, magnificent granite cliffs, wrecks, caverns, and tunnels. Divers of all levels will find Phuket diving to be a delight.

Beautiful underwater vistas are produced by bouncing coral gardens and boulder formations. The incredible diversity seen in these mostly unaltered habitats ranges from giant pelagic species like manta rays, whale sharks, and tuna to microscopic macro-animals like seahorses, ghost pipefish, and harlequin shrimp.

Lam Ru National Park is located on the northernmost point of Phuket's coastline and features a number of granitic outcrops in deep, clear water with reefs that drop to depths of 35 meters and below. The Similan Islands are what these are called.

## When to dive in Phuket

Due to its warm water, which never drops below 77°F/25°C, Phuket invites divers all year long. Plan your vacation to coincide with the months of November through May, when diving is permitted in the National Marine Park. 25–40 m is the range of visibility.

Since the majority of Phuket's dive sites are close to the coast and offer shore entrance or just need a brief transport by speedboat or longtail boat, accessibility is rarely impacted by the seasons. Sites are appropriate for all skill levels because currents are typically mild year-round.

Get lost in a fresh cast of creatures once the day has set and the moon is high in the sky. A diving location is transformed into an exotic world by the moonlight, complete with brilliant plankton and nocturnal marine life. All throughout the year, there are night dives that let you see your favorite places from a completely different angle.

## Zip-lining and Water Sports

Phuket offers a wide range of thrilling activities and is known for more than just its beautiful beaches and colorful culture. Look no farther than zip-lining and water activities if you're looking for an adrenaline rush and a chance to see the island's natural beauty in a novel way.

### Zip-lining Adventures

A heart-pounding adventure that provides a bird's-eye perspective of the island's magnificent sceneries is zip-lining through Phuket's lush jungles. As you soar over the treetops and across ravines while wearing a harness, you can take in expansive views of the Andaman Sea. On the island, there are a number of zip-lining sites and businesses that welcome both novice and seasoned thrill seekers. With qualified guides assuring a safe and thrilling ride, safety is given top attention.

## Water Sports

Phuket is the perfect playground for lovers of water sports due to its clean waters and mild environment. There is something for everyone, whether you are an expert or a novice:

Scuba diving: The undersea beauty of Phuket is known. Discover unusual marine creatures, explore beautiful coral reefs, and even dive at night to experience the nocturnal delights of the ocean.

Snorkeling: Snorkeling is a great way to explore the vibrant underwater world for a more laid-back aquatic vacation. There are several locations where snorkeling is possible, including Coral Island and the Similan Islands.

a jet ski: As you cruise across the waves on a jet ski, experience the exhilaration of the wide ocean. Many beaches have rental companies accessible, so you can easily get in the water.

Parasailing is when you ride on a speedboat's tow and soar above the water. You won't forget the thrill of parasailing, which offers a distinctive viewpoint of Phuket's coastline.

Catching the wind and riding the waves are two things you can do with windsurfing and kitesurfing. Nai Harn and Kata beaches in Phuket provide ideal conditions for these activities.

Paddleboarding: With paddleboarding, you may take your time discovering tranquil coves and mangrove forests on the ocean.

Kayaking: By kayaking throughout Phuket's coastline, you can find undiscovered lagoons, caves, and beaches. For those searching for an adventure with local knowledge, guided excursions are offered.

Flyboarding: Strap on a flyboard and soar above the water to take water sports to new heights. In little time at all, skilled instructors will have you pulling off tricks.

**Safety First**

Safety should always come first when partaking in these exciting activities. To get the most out of your zip-lining and water-sports adventures, make sure you listen to the advice of qualified instructors, utilize the appropriate gear, and observe safety precautions.

Phuket's zip-lining and water sports choices guarantee a memorable journey that will leave you with treasured memories of your time on this beautiful island, from the adrenaline of zipping through the treetops to the peace of exploring underwater worlds.

# Chapter five: Entertainment and Nightlife
## Bangla Street

The streets of Thailand come to life at night with lights, music, and enjoyable parties. Bangla Road, which is found in the beach resort town of Patong in the province of Phuket, is one of the best places for nightlife in the nation. Bangla Road, one of Patong's most popular attractions, is also known as Patong Walking Street. There are other sois (side streets) along the 400-meter-long route that are also involved in the celebration.

Bangla road-Party atmosphere

## How to Get to Bangla Road

On Phuket Island's southwest shore, close to the stunning Andaman Sea, is where you'll find Bangla Road. By automobile, it takes around an hour to get to Phuket International Airport. It would take between 35 and 45 minutes to get to Bangla Road from Phuket Town.

Additionally, there are several open-sided or contemporary air-conditioned bus services that run between Phuket

Town and Patong. The standard bus price is 10 baht. There are three primary locations where passengers may board a bus: Central Market Terminal on Ranong Road, Phuket Bus Terminal One on Phang Nga Road, and Phuket Bus Terminal Two on Thepkasattri Road. In Patong, buses stop at Jungceylon Shopping Mall, which is close to Bangla Road.

Visitors may also be able to go to Patong by taking a songthaew, which is a truck or other large vehicle that has been converted into a little bus. The average cost of a songthaew ride is 15 baht, and there is no set schedule for songthaew service. Look for the destination of the car, which is typically written on the front or side windows. When you flag it down, it will stop for a pickup.

Bangla road-Party in a nightclub

## First-Time Visitors: Expectations on Bangla Road
Bangla Road is a unique place to spend a night out. Having a brief rundown of what to anticipate might be beneficial for people who are visiting for the first time. While there are several pubs and clubs lining the streets, the party always overflows into the streets.

On three sides, almost all of the bars and clubs along the strip lack walls in favor of a covered roof. Tourists visiting the walking street may anticipate hearing a variety of musical genres because of how open they are.

Instead of staying at one bar all night, most travelers choose to spend the evening bar hopping to locate the finest events.

Different styles of live music are performed in certain locations, while local and international dance music is played by D.J.s in other locations.

The atmosphere is further enhanced by neon lights, billboards, televisions, and colorful home accents that line the roadway.

The various pubs and nightclubs frequently have staff members outside enticing customers inside. They could discuss the night's entertainment lineup or announce their drink specials. Tourists shouldn't feel compelled to enter if they are simply passing by because there is only a little healthy competition amongst the bars for clients.

Tourists can expect to encounter both solitary and group street entertainers throughout the night. Breakdancing, magic acts, fire breathing, and other stunts could be included in their shows. To show appreciation for and support of the artists, think about adding money to the tip jar.

Alcoholic beverages on Bangla Road

## Bangla Road Nightclubs & Bars

On Patong Walking Street, there are so many different pubs and clubs to select from. Some are laid-back sports bars or beach bars with inexpensive drinks and excellent music, but no live entertainment. Other clubs include go-go dancers dancing directly on the bar top or a small stage area for dancers and vocalists. The easiest approach to appreciate Bangla Road's greatest features is to sample a few different bars' ambiances while having a drink there. It's crucial to remember that some of the most well-known places do need a cover fee to enter.

## Bars and clubs on Bangla Road you can't miss

1. Phuket's Illuzion This popular nightlife location in Thailand has three sizable rooms that can accommodate a huge number of trevelers. Popular house music is played by a number of resident D.J.s, and aerial performers also bring a little enchantment to the event. Internationally known DJs are occasionally hosted by Illuzion Phuket for special performances. The lively nightclub is open every day till one in the morning.

2. Tiger Nightclub: To find the Tiger Nightclub on Bangla Road, simply look for the enormous concrete tigers that

protrude from the building's second story. The complex's first level is home to a number of beer bars and loud techno music. A tranquil space called the Tiger Pool Club is also available for guests to relax in and play a game of pool while sipping a beverage. Tiger Disco, a sizable dance club adorned with tiger sculptures, occupies the most of the upper levels. This nightclub is a terrific spot to dance and has local and international D.J.s. Everyday till 4:00 AM, it is open.

3. White Room Nightclub is a well-liked nightclub with a contemporary all-white décor. It is located on Patong Walking Street. This club has a smart casual dress code, despite the fact that other places on the strip are more laid back. The V.I.P area is a lively and elegant setting where you may dress up and enjoy a Thai beer, a tropical cocktail, or bottle service. The diverse music that the local and international DJs play is ideal for dancing. The club is open from Monday through Saturday until three in the morning and on Sundays until midnight.

4. Monsoon: Monsoon is the best pub in Phuket for live music. Upbeat music is provided on the main floor every night until approximately 2:00 AM by the Monsoon House Band. Until the pub shuts at 4:00 AM, revelers can either stay downstairs or go up to the

second level to play pool tables. Additionally well-known at Monsoon are its nightly inexpensive beer deals and its menu of classic western dishes including burgers and nachos.

## Where to Eat on Bangla Road

Tourists will probably want to grab a quick bite to eat before returning to their hotels after a hard night of drinking and dancing. With a whole soi dedicated to street cuisine, Bangla Road sellers are ready to satisfy any desires. This area is open every day from 6:00 PM to 1:00 AM and is referred to as the Bangla Night Market.

At Bangla Night Market, you may get both traditional Thai food and food from other countries.

Fried rice bowls, fresh seafood platters, meat and veggie skewers, stir-fries, and even French fries and fried chicken are a few of the menu items that are quite popular.

Additionally, there are many of sweet options available, including crepes, Thai sticky rice, and folded ice cream.

Visitors can also purchase a beverage to accompany their meal. There are several vendors offering fresh fruit juices, smoothies, and other refreshments, as well as wine and other alcoholic beverages.

Expect to pay around 200 baht for a full meal.

Try to take a seat at one of the tables after making an order and enjoying some delectable street cuisine. Although there are many tables and foldable chairs accessible, they do become congested during particular hours of the night.

# Wildlife Encounters

## Elephant Sanctuaries

A trip to an elephant sanctuary in Phuket is a popular destination for tourists. A rare opportunity to engage with Thailand's rich cultural heritage and natural beauty is to interact with these mighty animals up close. But it's critical to select ethical and responsible refuges that put elephant welfare ahead of commercial exploitation.

## A Turning Toward Ethical Travel

The treatment of elephants in Phuket and throughout Thailand's tourism industry has improved in recent years. Instead of traditional elephant riding or performances, which sometimes entail unethical methods, many tourists are now choosing sanctuaries that place a strong emphasis on the wellbeing of these gentle giants.

## What to Expect at Elephant Sanctuaries

Following are common activities when visiting an ethical elephant sanctuary in Phuket:

Visitors may view elephants in their natural habitat, interact with them by feeding them, and learn about their behavior and history. The only real interactions were feeding, washing, and politely spending time with the elephants.

Educational Programs: Ethical sanctuaries offers educational programs that shed light on the difficulties that elephants in Thailand confront as well as the significance of conservation efforts.

Bathing Rituals: Taking a mud bath and a river bath with the elephants is one of the most enjoyable experiences. It's a chance to observe these creatures respectfully swimming around in the water while having fun.

Visitors may take part in feeding sessions when they can give the elephants their favorite foods, such bananas, sugarcane, and watermelons.

Learning About Conservation: Ethical sanctuaries frequently feature informed workers who give information about elephant conservation and initiatives to save these majestic animals from overexploitation and habitat destruction.

## The Importance of Ethical Sanctuaries

It's crucial to select an ethical elephant sanctuary for various reasons:

Pet welfare: Elephants' welfare is given top priority in ethical sanctuaries, which prevent them from engaging in damaging activities like riding or performing feats.

Elephant conservation: Many sanctuaries actively support efforts to save elephants by saving mistreated or abandoned elephants and giving them a loving home.

Education: These refuges are essential in spreading knowledge about the difficulties faced by elephants in Thailand and throughout the world.

Supporting moral elephant sanctuaries aids in promoting ethical, responsible, and sustainable tourist activities, which benefits nearby communities and protects natural environments.

Responsible Visitor Guidelines

The following ethical principles must be followed when visiting an elephant sanctuary:

Observe from a Safe Distance: Be mindful of the elephants' privacy and keep your distance when watching them.

To guarantee the safety of both people and elephants, pay attention to the directions of sanctuary employees and guides.

No Performance or Riding: Pick sanctuaries where there are no shows or opportunities for riding elephants because these things might be bad for the animals.

Stay away from single-use plastics: By staying away from single-use plastics and disposing of garbage appropriately, you may lessen your influence on the environment.

By selecting ethical elephant sanctuaries in Phuket, you can support responsible and sustainable tourism methods that benefit both the elephants and the local community. You can also contribute to the welfare of these majestic animals.

## Phuket Aquarium

The Phuket Aquarium, which houses hundreds of tropical, colorful, and unique aquatic species, provides a wonderful afternoon for the entire family. Children who may not have previously had the opportunity to get up close and personal with such exotic marine species enjoy the Aquarium.

Children may spend a lot of time being amazed by the strangeness of the underwater world thanks to the more than 30 tanks of freshwater and saltwater animals. The so-ugly-you-can't-help-staring stonefish could have no other name, whereas cuttlefish hover like spaceships, razorfish like sinking sticks, and stonefish appear like cuttlefish. Eels, crabs, shrimp, sharks, and fish with colors ranging from spectacular to deceptively subtle are among the varied assortment.

Phuket Aquarium, one of the attractions, Phuket's Top 67 Activities and Phuket's Top 10 Activities When It Pours (Read more here about the Phuket Province.)

**The Phuket Aquarium's tunnel**

The main draw is a large tank with a tunnel running through it. A multicolored swarm of rays, snapper, grouper, wrasse, sharks, and other fish surround you within. For an added bonus, arrive at lunchtime, say at 11am on the weekends, to see the fish eating. The 110-ton tank at the aquarium is home to enormous fish that are the size of men when you emerge from the tunnel.

All displays include labels in both Thai and English that give fascinating information about the animals. Greater detail is provided regarding marine creatures, ecosystems, and conservation challenges via floor-to-ceiling wall displays. A natural walk outside the main museum leads to several turtles. Baby hawksbill and green sea turtles can be found practicing their swimming skills in large pools, while wounded adults can retire early in the rehabilitation area.

Phuket Aquarium is a component of the Phuket Marine Biological Center (PMBC), an 8-hectare site on Phuket's southeast coast that is dedicated to marine teaching, research, and conservation.

# Chapter six: Cuisine and Dining

Eating Thai food is a huge (and critical) part of any journey to Bangkok and Thailand. Thai food is well-liked all around the world because of its unusual flavors and aromas. When exploring the city's alleyways, it's common to come across food stalls where, for very cheap costs, you can eat skewered meats, fried rice, noodles, and spicy soups.

Many restaurants in Bangkok provide a wide selection of traditional Thai foods if you'd rather eat in a more cozy environment. Consult our list of the greatest Thai restaurants to sample the best regional cuisine the city has to offer.

## Must-Try Dishes

### Spicy shrimp soup

Tom yum goong

Aromatic lemongrass, chillies, galangal, kaffir lime leaves, shallots, lime juice, and fish sauce are combined in the robust, reviving dish tom yum goong. This hot and sour soup, which includes straw mushrooms and delicious river shrimp, is best served with steaming white rice.

Spicy green papaya salad

Som tum

Som tum, or hot green papaya salad, originated in the northern Thai province of Isaan. Using a pestle and mortar, garlic, chillies, green beans, cherry tomatoes, and shredded raw papaya are crushed to create a characteristic sweet-sour-spicy flavor. In some regions, the mixture may also contain peanuts, dried shrimp, or salted crab. Some people can't get enough of the flavor of this meal, while others can't stand the spiciness.

### Chicken in coconut soup
Tom kha kai

Tom kha kai, a milder variation on tom yum, combines hot peppers, finely sliced young galangal, crushed shallots, stalks of lemongrass, and delicate chicken pieces. Before the meal is finished with fresh lime leaves, coconut milk is added to the recipe to tone down the spice. Steamed rice goes well with a bowl of creamy tom kha kai, as it does with most Thai-style soups.

### Red curry
Gaeng daeng

Gaeng daeng is a flavorful red curry dish that includes meat, creamy coconut milk, red curry paste, and sliced kaffir lime leaves on top. Gaeng daeng, despite its eye-catching color, is actually rather moderate; nevertheless, if you're in the mood for hot cuisine, you can ask for fresh chilli. By requesting the cook to substitute tofu for the beef, vegetarians or vegans can still enjoy this curry.

## Thai-style fried noodles
Pad Thai

One of Thailand's most well-known meals is pad Thai. Small, thin or broad noodles are stir-fried in a blistering hot wok with onion, egg, crisp beansprouts, and other ingredients. Additionally, ingredients including fish sauce, dried shrimp, garlic or shallots, red chilli, and palm sugar are used to flavor the meal. Pad thai is normally made with fresh shrimp, crab, or squid, but some places also provide chicken, beef, or pork. A wedge of lime, crushed roasted peanuts, bean sprouts, and fresh herbs are frequently placed on the dish with the stir-fried noodles.

## Fried rice
Khao pad

In Bangkok, khao pad, or fried rice, is frequently eaten during lunch. You may simply add additional ingredients to this straightforward rice, egg, and onion dish, such as prawns, crab, or chicken, as well as tofu, basil, or leftover veggies.

## Stir-fried basil and pork
Pad krapow moo

You may have pad krapow moo, a Thai meal, for lunch or supper. A wok is used to stir-fry minced pork, holy basil leaves, huge fresh chillies, pork, green beans, soy sauce, and sugar. A fried egg (kai dao) is placed on top of the cooked mixture and heaped high on a bed of steaming white rice.

## Green chicken curry
Gaeng keow wan kai

Despite having components that are typical of Thai curries, gaeng keow wan kai has a distinctive color because to green chillies. Coconut milk, cherry-sized eggplants, bamboo shoots, galangal, lemongrass, coriander, and fragrant basil are all ingredients in this green chicken curry. With flatbread or steamed rice, it tastes richer and sweeter than the traditional tom yum.

## Spicy beef salad
Yum nua

Yum nua is a light Thai salad with delicate beef pieces on top. It utilizes a tangy dressing consisting of lime juice, palm sugar, sesame oil, ginger, garlic, and fish sauce. Yum nua can be enjoyed on its own, although rice helps to temper the dish's sour-sweet flavor.

## Stir-fried chicken with cashew nuts
Kai pad med ma muang

In essence, chicken and cashews are stir-fried in kai pad med ma muang. Along with a variety of veggies (often chopped bell peppers or carrots), this meal also includes soy sauce, honey, onions, chilies, and pepper. Although there are dried chillies mixed in with the cashew nuts and chicken, the dish is rarely hot. Children or anyone who can't take hot cuisine should eat this meal.

# Street Food Delights

It's simple to overlook the fact that Thai cuisine is uniquely regional, a patchwork of ingredients, recipes, and preparation methods that have been modified and developed over hundreds of years under the influence of invaders, spice routes, and merchant traders. In traditional Phuketian cuisine, a culinary mash-up influenced by Hakka and Hokkien, Malay and Indian, most of the food we associate with Thai cuisine doesn't exist. A large portion of Phuket's cuisine is made with recipes that have been handed down through generations of Peranakans, mixed-race descendants of Southern Chinese who immigrated to the island during the 16th century tin mining boom and married locals.

Therefore, skip the pad krapow stir fry, tom yum goong soup, and som tam papaya salad. Also skip the gaeng kiew wan green Thai curry. If you can force yourself off the island's sun-drenched sand, you'll discover an intricate and nuanced world of island cooking, a fusion of flavors from all over Asia, with recipes so significant that the food has been given UNESCO gastronomy status. This is a world that is definitely worth exploring.

## Hokkien mee (หมี่ฮกเกี้ยน)

platters of seafood Hokkien mee at Go La / Streets of Food with shrimp and soft-boiled eggs

Like many of Phuket's popular street foods, hokkien mee is authentically named after its native country. In a salty, smoky sauce consisting of soy, white pepper, and pig broth cooked in fiercely hot woks, are chewy egg noodles, reddish-tinged char siu barbecue pork, delicately blanched rings of squid and prawns, and Chinese cabbage. A soft poached egg is recommended because its runny yolk gives the noodles a glossier finish and emulsifies into a creamier sauce. Families from Bangkok who are on vacation gravitate toward this bowl first.

**Go La, 1 Kra Road, Tambon Talat Ya, Phuket 83000, to sample Hokkien mee while you're in Phuket.**

Loba (โลบะ)

The dish loba divides opinion among visitors. There is no dodging the unsightly dish of fried pig parts, which includes tofu that, after being cooked in the same oil as the offal it is tossed with, is about as vegetarian as the offal it is tossed with. Despite its Hokkien roots, it is a popular snack in Phuket. A variety of textures, including chewy, crunchy, and soft, can be found beneath the surface of the fried food. These textures are bound together by the flavors of Chinese five spice and a tart, pungent sauce made of tamarind, palm sugar, and chilli. The adventurous have lunch or a mid-morning snack with the locals.

**Loba Bang Niao is located at 18/61 Mae Luan Road, Talad Nuea, Phuket, 83000.**

Moo hong (หมูฮ้อง)

If there is one dish that best represents Phuketian cuisine, it is called moo hong. This Peranakan favorite combines Southern Chinese flavors with island flavors, ingredients, and cooking methods that are prevalent in Phuket cuisine. Each family's well guarded recipe begins with fatty pieces of pork belly cooked in garlic and palm sugar, crushed coriander root and black peppercorns, star anise, and soy sauce. Some are dark and intensely savory, while others are sticky and sweet. Without causing the pig to lose its shape, the flesh is cooked just long enough to become tender and the fat and skin to become soft and gelatinous.

**Visit Raya Restaurant at 48/1 Dibuk Road, Tambon Talat Yai, Phuket 83000 if you want to sample moo hong sod there.**

Popiah sod (ปอเปี๊ยสด)

Thai spring rolls, those crispy, golden torpedos stuffed with veggies and bean sprouts, are a takeout favorite. Popiah sod, a popular street dish in Phuket that is made in the Fujian manner, is less well known, which is unfortunate because they are far more intricate and intriguing than its deep-fried relatives. Both were introduced by Chinese immigrants a century ago; neither is Thai in origin. Although the filling varies across sellers, the wafer-thin crepe-like wrapper is formed by rolling elastic dough over a hot plate. At its center, however, are usually pieces of kun chiang (cured Chinese sausage), crunchy bean sprouts, soft tofu, and shredded omelette with just a bit preserved radish. Some people spoon in the delicate crab flesh while others add toasted peanuts or crispy pig skin for texture.

No one is spared from the sweet, gooey soy and hoisin sauce's smothering.

**To taste popiah sod in Phuket, go to Lock Tien, 173 Yaowarat Road, Tambon Talat Nuea, Phuket 83000.**

Khua kling (คั่วกลิ้ง)

Khua kling () Although southern Thai cuisine is known for its scorching heat, nothing compares to the dish's ground chicken or pork, which is dry-fried and seasoned with curry paste, lemongrass, galangal, shredded kaffir lime leaves, and an uncountable number of Thai chillies. Despite the common assumption that good Thai food must be spicy, the only way to enjoy khua kling is with searing chilli heat. Something is wrong if the temperature does not cause your face to become numb and your cheeks to begin to perspire. Steamed jasmine rice served in a mound and thick slices of raw cabbage ease the discomfort.

To try khua kling in Phuket, visit: Mor Mu Dong, 9/4 Mu 3 Soi Pa Lai, Chao Fa Road, Chalong, Phuket, 83130

## Chapter seven: Practical information
## Staying safe in Phuket

- Water: Avoid drinking from the faucets. Use only bottled water.
- Ice is always manufactured with pure water and is completely safe.
- Mosquitoes: Although rare, dengue disease does occasionally arise in Phuket. Malaria is so uncommon that it practically doesn't exist. Utilize bug repellent and cover oneself at night to avoid getting bitten.
- Drugs: All drug-related offenses have very harsh punishments.
- Driving: Exercise extreme caution since collisions happen often.
- Dial 191 for police, 1155 for the tourist police, and 1669 for an ambulance in the event of an emergency.

## Local customs and etiquette

Temples: Wear proper clothing and make sure your legs are covered, at least to the knee. You should take off your shoes and hat before entering a temple.

Buddha: In Thailand, Buddha images are greatly revered. If you are not a Buddhist, purchasing sculptures and having

Buddhist tattoos are regarded as disrespectful and occasionally even illegal.

Royalty: Public criticism of Thailand's royal family is prohibited because of their tremendous regard for them. At 8 a.m. and 6 p.m., the national anthem is played on the radio and at a few public locations, as well as before films in theaters. It will be required of you to stand.

Feet: Making gestures with your feet is quite impolite.

Buddha Days: During certain religious holidays in Thailand, alcohol sales are prohibited.

Convenience stores only sell alcohol between the hours of 11 a.m. and 2 p.m. and between the hours of 5 p.m. and midnight. Except on religious and royal holidays, pubs and restaurants provide alcohol 24/7.

## Stay connected in Phuket

SIM cards: These are typically priced from 50 baht and are sold at the airport and convenience stores all across Phuket. To register the number, you must present your passport.

Power supply: 220 volts at 50 hertz. Plugs of types A, B, and C (USA style).

# Money and Currency Exchange

Thailand's most well-known tourist resort, Phuket, utilizes the Thai Baht (THB) as its official unit of exchange. Here are some important considerations to have in mind about money and currency conversion in Phuket:

Money: The Thai Baht is denoted by the symbol and is abbreviated as THB.

Exchange rates: Because they might differ from one exchange provider to another, it's a good idea to compare rates before choosing one. The most recent currency rates are available online and in banks and exchange offices in Phuket.

Where to Exchange Money: Banks, currency exchange offices, and some hotels are just a few locations in Phuket where you may exchange money. Banks often provide competitive rates, however their hours of operation may be restricted. Although they frequently stay open later, particularly on weekends, currency exchange offices and booths may provide somewhat worse prices. Avoid changing money at the airport since the exchange rates there are frequently worse.

ATMs: There are several ATMs in tourist locations in Phuket, which has a well-developed network of them.

ATMs allow you to withdraw Thai Baht with a debit or credit card. Always verify currency rates and costs for foreign withdrawals with your bank. To avoid any problems, confirm that your card is compatible internationally and let your bank know about your vacation intentions.

Credit Cards: In bigger places like hotels, upscale restaurants, and stores, credit cards are routinely accepted. Cash, however, could be the favored means of payment in smaller or more localized locations. Although American Express and other cards may also be accepted, Visa and MasterCard are the most frequently used.

Apps for currency exchange: To monitor exchange rates and convert currencies, you may also think about utilizing apps for currency exchange. When utilizing applications or services for online currency conversion, use caution to assure their security and dependability.

Thai Baht is available in a range of denominations, including coins of 1, 2, 5, and 10 Baht, as well as notes worth 20, 50, 100, 500, and 1,000 Baht.

Exchange Old or Damaged Bills: Some locations might not take old or torn bills, so make sure you have clean, undamaged bills when exchanging money.

As you would in any tourist location, be cautious when handling and exchanging money in Phuket. Pay attention to conversion rates, refrain from carrying large sums of cash, and take the appropriate safety measures to protect your money and financial data.

## Getting around Phuket
# Transportation in Phuket

Transportation in Phuket: Getting around Phuket is relatively easy, thanks to various transportation options available. Here's what you need to know:

- Taxis: Taxis are a convenient way to travel around Phuket. They may be hailed from the street or found at taxi stands. Ensure that the meter is used or negotiate the fare before starting the journey. Taxis in Phuket are usually color-coded, with red and yellow being the most common.

- Tuk-tuks: Tuk-tuks are three-wheeled motorized vehicles that are a popular mode of transportation in Phuket. They are often brightly decorated and offer a unique and fun way to get around. However, fares are usually negotiated, so be prepared to haggle and agree on a price before hopping on.

- Motorbike Taxis: If you're traveling alone or with a companion and want a quicker way to navigate through traffic, motorbike taxis are a popular option. They can be found at designated stands and are recognized by their colored vests. Negotiate the fare in advance and don't forget to wear a helmet for safety.

- Rental Scooters: Renting a scooter is a popular choice for many visitors in Phuket. It allows for more flexibility and the freedom to explore the island at your own pace. However, make sure you have the necessary driving license, wear a helmet, and exercise caution while driving, as traffic conditions can be challenging.

- Songthaews are modified pickup trucks that have covered seats in the rear. They serve as shared taxis or mini-buses, following specific routes around the island. Look for the color-coded signs indicating the destinations they serve. Songthaews are an affordable option for short to medium distances.

- Public Buses: Phuket also has a public bus system that connects various parts of the island. The buses are relatively inexpensive, but the routes and schedules may be less frequent or convenient for tourists. They can be a viable option if you're traveling on a budget or prefer a more local experience.

- Car Rental: Renting a car is an excellent choice if you prefer the convenience of having your own vehicle. Several car rental companies operate in Phuket, and having a car allows you to explore the island more independently. Ensure you have a valid driver's license and be aware of the traffic rules and driving conditions.

- Grab and Other Ride-Hailing Apps: Grab, a popular ride-hailing app in Southeast Asia, operates in Phuket. It offers convenient and transparent pricing for taxi rides, making it a reliable option for transportation.

**Rental Agencies in Phuket:**

Avis: With a location in Phuket, Avis is a well-known international vehicle rental company. They provide a range of automobiles and frequently provide excellent customer service.

Budget: Operating in Phuket, Budget Car Rental provides a variety of vehicles at various pricing points.

Hertz is an additional worldwide rental company with operations in Phuket. They have several pick-up locations and a selection of automobiles available.

Local Companies: There are a number of local vehicle rental companies in Phuket that may provide affordable rates. Simply remember to read reviews and be informed about the terms and circumstances when working with neighborhood agencies.

Online platforms: You may compare costs from several rental providers, both local and foreign, using websites like Rentalcars.com, Expedia, or Kayak.

To get the cheapest costs, check rates from multiple companies and reserve in advance. Keep in mind that pricing might vary depending on the kind of car, the length of the rental, and the season. To avoid any unforeseen fees, always thoroughly read the rental agreement before signing.

# Phuket Safety and Health Tips

Thailand's Phuket is a well-liked vacation spot because of its magnificent beaches, exciting nightlife, and extensive cultural history. The following safety and health advice should be kept in mind to ensure a fun and safe trip:

## General Safety Tips:

- Invest in comprehensive travel insurance that includes emergency evacuation and medical coverage. This is essential in the event of unanticipated illnesses or accidents.
- Maintain Your Hydration: Phuket's weather can be hot and muggy. Stay hydrated by drinking lots of water, especially if you're spending time outside.
- Cross the street with caution in order to maintain traffic safety. Use pedestrian crossings whenever possible, and always be alert of your surroundings because Thai traffic may be quite hectic.
- Petty Theft: Take care of your possessions, especially in busy places and popular tourist destinations. Carry your valuables in a neck bag or money belt.
- Beach Safety: Pay attention to lifeguard warnings. Strong currents may be present at some beaches. Be

cautious of jellyfish and only swim in approved places, especially during specific seasons.

- Sun protection: To shield oneself from the intense tropical sun, put on sunscreen, sunglasses, and a hat. Especially if you've been swimming, reapply sunscreen.

The majority of Thai people are amiable, however it's necessary to respect their culture and traditions. When visiting temples, dress modestly and take off your shoes before entering places of worship.

## Health Tips:

- Avoid drinking tap water and using ice cubes in your beverages. To lower your chance of contacting foodborne diseases, stick with bottled water and dine at popular, trustworthy establishments.
- Verify that all of your usual vaccines are current. For advice on recommended travel vaccinations, including those for Hepatitis A and Typhoid, speak with your doctor.
- Protection against mosquitoes: Phuket is located in an area where illnesses spread by mosquitoes, like as dengue fever, are common. Wear long sleeves, long trousers, and insect repellant, especially at night and throughout the evening.

- Find the location of the closest hospital or clinic under "Medical Facilities." Always keep a first aid kit on hand, along with any essential prescription drugs.
- COVID-19 Precautions: Keep up with the most recent COVID-19 recommendations, and adhere to the suggested safety precautions, which include using masks in crowded areas and washing your hands often.
- Animal Safety: To prevent bites or scratches, stay away from petting or approaching stray or strange animals.
- Prescription drugs should be brought on trips in their original containers along with a copy of the prescription.

By adhering to these health and safety recommendations, you may visit Phuket with ease and concentrate on the stunning surroundings and many cultural experiences the island has to offer.

## Useful Thai Phrases

For visitors or anybody interested in learning some basic Thai, here are some helpful Thai phrases with their English translations:

- Hello: สวัสดี (sawasdee)
- Goodbye: ลาก่อน (laa kawn)
- Yes: ใช่ (chai)

- No: ไม่ (mai)
- Thank you: ขอบคุณ (khob khun)
- Sorry/Excuse me: ขอโทษ (khor toht)
- Please: โปรด (proht)
- How are you?: คุณสบายดีไหม (kun sabai dee mai?)
- What is your name?: คุณชื่ออะไร (kun cheu arai?)
- My name is [your name]: ฉันชื่อ [your name] (chan cheu [your name])
- I don't understand: ฉันไม่เข้าใจ (chan mai khao jai)
- Where is the restroom?: ห้องน้ำอยู่ที่ไหน (hawng nahm yoo tee nai?)
- How much is this?: นี่เท่าไหร่ (nee tao rai?)
- Water: น้ำ (nahm)
- Food: อาหาร (ah-han)
- Help: ช่วยด้วย (chûai dûay)
- I need a doctor: ฉันต้องการหมอ (chan dtong gaan mor)
- I'm lost: ฉันหลงทาง (chan long tang)
- Can you speak English?: คุณพูดภาษาอังกฤษได้ไหม (kun poot paa-saa ang-grit dai mai?)
- I love Thailand: ฉันรักประเทศไทย (chan rak pra-teet Thai)

Just keep in mind that Thai is a tonal language, so the way you utter a word might affect its meaning. To learn the correct tones, it may be beneficial to practice with a native speaker or a language-learning program.

# 7 days itineraries

### Day 1: Arrival in Phuket

- **Morning:** Arrive at Phuket International Airport. Check into your chosen accommodation.
- **Afternoon:** Relax and rejuvenate on Patong Beach, famous for its golden sands and vibrant atmosphere.
- **Evening:** Stroll along Bangla Road for shopping, dining, and experiencing Phuket's bustling nightlife.

### Day 2: Island Hopping

- **Morning:** Embark on a day trip to Phi Phi Islands. Enjoy snorkeling, swimming, and exploring the stunning Maya Bay.
- **Evening:** Return to Phuket. Enjoy a seafood dinner at Rawai Beach.

### Day 3: Cultural Exploration

- **Morning:** Visit Wat Chalong, the largest Buddhist temple in Phuket.
- **Afternoon:** Explore the historic Old Phuket Town with its colorful Sino-Portuguese architecture.
- **Evening:** Try local street food at the Phuket Sunday Night Market.

### Day 4: Adventure and Nature

- **Morning:** Head to Phang Nga Bay and kayak through limestone caves and emerald waters.
- **Afternoon:** Visit the Elephant Sanctuary for an ethical encounter with these gentle giants.
- **Evening:** Return to your hotel for relaxation.

### Day 5: Beach Bliss and Water Sports

- **Morning:** Spend a relaxing morning at Karon Beach, known for its tranquility.
- **Afternoon:** Engage in water sports at Kata Beach, including surfing or paddleboarding.
- **Evening:** Enjoy a sunset dinner at Promthep Cape, offering breathtaking views.

### Day 6: Explore the Northern Coast

- **Morning:** Visit the Big Buddha, a towering icon that offers panoramic views of the island.
- **Afternoon:** Explore Phuket's northern beaches, such as Kamala Beach and Surin Beach.
- **Evening:** Savor a seafood dinner at a beachfront restaurant.

### Day 7: Farewell to Phuket

- **Morning:** Visit the Gibbon Rehabilitation Project and learn about conservation efforts.

- **Afternoon:** Spend your last hours shopping in Patong or getting a traditional Thai massage.
- **Evening:** Enjoy a farewell dinner at a beachfront restaurant, reflecting on your unforgettable week in Phuket.

# Conclusion

We want to thank you from the bottom of our hearts for using our travel guide as your finest travel companion throughout your time in Phuket.

The words on these pages should have been more than just words; we want them to have been a call to action, a summons to immerse yourself in Phuket's unending beauty, to taste the tastes, to feel the sand beneath your toes, and to allow the spirit of this island to stir something deep inside of you.

Keep in mind the lively marketplaces, the frangipani aroma, and the kind grins of the residents. Recall the excitement of discovery and the calm of sunset moments. You may now save these memories as a reminder that the world is big and that a fresh chapter is ready to be written around every turn.

Carry Phuket with you when you step out of these pages and into the world. Inspire yourself on your own adventure with the tenacity of its people, the depth of its culture, and the beauty of its landscapes. Accept the wonder you've found here and allow it to inspire your curiosity, generosity, and bravery.

There comes a time in every voyage when you realize how big and little the world is, and how other people's experiences may influence your own. We hope that this guide has provided you with such a moment, one that opens your heart to the wonders of the world and the amazing tales it still has to tell.

We appreciate you allowing us to participate in your research, dear reader. Wishing you a journey full of unending amazement, deep relationships, and the unwavering conviction that the world is, in fact, a magnificent work of art just waiting to be discovered.

# PHUKET

*Travel journal*

*This journal belongs to*

NAME _____

PHONE NO _____

ADDRESS _____

_____

_____

# TRAVEL TO:

Destination

Date

Place to see

Notes

_____
_____
_____
_____

Place to see

_____
_____
_____
_____

Place to see

_____
_____
_____
_____

# TRAVEL CHECK LIST

| CLOTTHING | TOILETRIES |
|---|---|
| | |
| | |
| | |
| | |
| | |

| CARRY ON | OTHER THINGS |
|---|---|
| | |
| | |
| | |
| | |
| | |

# MY BUDGET

| DESCRIPTION | COST |
|---|---|
| | |
| | |
| | |
| | |
| | |
| | |
| | |
| | |
| | |
| | |
| | |
| | |
| | |
| | |
| | |
| | |
| | |
| | |
| | |

# TRIP ITINERARY

| DAY 1 | DAY 2 |
|-------|-------|
|       |       |
|       |       |
|       |       |
|       |       |
|       |       |
|       |       |
|       |       |
|       |       |
|       |       |
|       |       |
|       |       |
|       |       |
|       |       |

# TRIP ITINERARY

| DAY 3 | DAY 4 |
|-------|-------|
|       |       |
|       |       |
|       |       |
|       |       |
|       |       |
|       |       |
|       |       |
|       |       |
|       |       |
|       |       |
|       |       |
|       |       |
|       |       |
|       |       |

# TRIP ITINERARY

| DAY 5 | DAY 6 |
| --- | --- |
| | |
| | |
| | |
| | |
| | |
| | |
| | |
| | |
| | |
| | |
| | |
| | |
| | |

# TRIP ITINERARY

| DAY 7 | DAY 8 |
|-------|-------|
|       |       |
|       |       |
|       |       |
|       |       |
|       |       |
|       |       |
|       |       |
|       |       |
|       |       |
|       |       |
|       |       |
|       |       |
|       |       |
|       |       |
|       |       |

# MEMORIES/EXPERIENCE

## NOTE

# MEMORIES/EXPERIENCE

## NOTE

# MEMORIES/EXPERIENCE

## NOTE

Printed in Great Britain
by Amazon